T0129099

PLEASE LET IT BE
ENOUGH

YESHIL KOHL

ARCHWAY
PUBLISHING

Archway Publishing books may be ordered
through booksellers or by contacting:

Archway Publishing
1663 Liberty Drive
Bloomington, IN 47403
www.archwaypublishing.com
1 (888) 242-5904

ISBN: 978-1-4808-7274-5 (sc)
ISBN: 978-1-4808-7275-2 (e)

Library of Congress Control Number: 2018966443

Print information available on the last page.

Archway Publishing rev. date: 01/16/2019

CHAPTER ONE

Oh, no, she wants me to go with him again!

Oh, please, don't make me go, as I plead with my mother, and try to get her to understand what my father is going to do to me once we are alone in the car. My mother shoves me away and won't let me talk. I slowly realize that she knows, she knows, SHE KNOWS......and she wants him to sexually assault me. She just wants us both out of the house, so the young women coming for a shorthand class won't understand what is going on.

I had just had a severe beating with a broom handle, which left my arm paralyzed and dangling–can't let anybody see that. My parents' business school had gone bankrupt, but my mother was still teaching her shorthand class at home. That certainly took priority over any concern for me.

People wonder why victims of assault, both physical and sexual, wait for years to report it. I can tell you why. They are ashamed, embarrassed, afraid of the reaction of others, and they have lived with this for so long that it is a permanent part of them. It is never going away, but something triggers the need to get it off their backs in the vain hope that this will somehow make it go away. Maybe, just maybe, someone will understand and try to help.

Please let it be enough.

CHAPTER TWO

My parents never wanted children, but I came, anyway. I was born eleven days before Pearl Harbor, so my father (henceforth known as Carter) was drafted. He was sent to Norfolk, Virginia, for naval training. My mother (henceforth known as Ona) decided to go with him. She dumped me off with her parents in Tennessee, where I remained for a full year. I was never told about this stay. I always wondered why I felt so close to Grandpa Duncan, when I had never been around him much. Ona was a hoarder and her house was crammed with furniture, magazines, papers, etc. When I was in my 40's, I suddenly received a small package from her with an accompanying note that she had been cleaning house (?) The package contained several letters written from Grandma Duncan to Ona talking about me as a toddler, giving a report of how I was doing at their house. I was quoted as saying, "My Mommy is coming to get me." I was so shocked by the letter, that I was unable to read any of the other letters and I threw them all away.

A memory came back to me. Carter had been transferred to Seattle and my grandparents had apparently put pressure on

Ona to take me with her. Ona was a total stranger to me at that point. We both took a train from Tennessee to Seattle. It was a Pullman on which daytime seats were converted into berths at night, covered with curtains for privacy. For some unknown reason I was placed in an upper berth at one end of the car and my mother was somewhere at the other end. I became frightened and pulled back my curtain, intending to call Ona. Suddenly a large, black porter came in the door and started down the aisle. Having been raised in a segregated South, I had never seen a black person, so I backed off and waited till he was gone. Then I looked out again at that sea of curtains, and knew there was a strong possibility she wouldn't answer. At the tender age of two, I was faced with the realization that I was totally alone and I was always going to be. I cried myself to sleep.

Please let it be enough.

CHAPTER THREE

In this book, I made a conscious decision not to describe the sexual assault I endured. The only way I can describe it is to think about it. I don't WANT to think about it. It's upsetting enough to be discussing it in general.

There are two reasons why I am writing this book. Firstly, I am hoping it will involve catharsis, though I realize that is a very remote possibility. Secondly, I want to give a message to all my fellow sufferers—YOU ARE NOT ALONE. For many years I was convinced that I was the only person that this ever happened to—that everyone else had a Donna Reed type of family with everybody happy, loved and well cared for. It was only as the stories of others came out that I began to realize that this is an epidemic, a world-wide epidemic, that nobody is doing anything about. Knowledge is the beginning of action. I am hoping and praying that my little piece of knowledge will help in bringing victims out of the shadows and the problem into the light.

Assaulters are rarely prosecuted. How many times have you heard the argument that there were no witnesses? What kind of an idiot assaulter is going to look around, see that he has a good crowd of witnesses and THEN decides to commit his crime? On the contrary, they look for times and places where they will NOT be seen. If a victim has gone through the agony of both being attacked AND coming out into public to deal with what in effect is a second assault, you MUST LISTEN and try to make his/her ordeal a little easier.

CHAPTER FOUR

When I was a child, we moved often–usually about once a year. Nobody ever explained anything to me, but since Carter's bipolar illness caused him to be out of work a lot, I am assuming that we were probably evicted for not paying the rent. Each time we moved, we always left behind at least one cat. I would cry and plead, but my mother wouldn't even discuss it. As an adult, I have always had cats, as do all my children, and they are treated like family.

When I was five and six, we rented a house in my home town, which belonged to snowbirds, which were people who lived in Florida in the winter and moved back north in the summer heat. This meant that we lived in their house all winter and had to get out in the summer. For two summers we lived with Carter's parents ten miles from town. My grandparents Elton ran a country inn in the summer accommodating about 30 snowbirds. Grandma was an excellent country cook and Grandpa ran a farm and apple orchard, raising most of the food Grandma cooked. My mother reluctantly worked to help Grandma, and Grandpa cleaned out an old chicken coop for us to live in, while Carter drove into town to work. I followed my taciturn Grandpa around all day, probably driving him nuts with questions. He got even with me twice. I had been begging him to let me ride the mule bareback, but he kept refusing without giving me a reason. Finally, he gave in and then I found out the reason–the mule's spine was like a razor blade cutting into my insides. I had too much pride to holler uncle, so I stuck it out.

Another time Grandpa said he was taking the wagon out to the woods to pick up wood for the fireplace. Again, I wore him down, because I loved to stand up in the wagon and balance during the bumpy ride. After Grandpa loaded up some fallen logs, I wanted to ride back on top of the logs. Grandpa said, no, but then gave in. Halfway back, I started to itch, and then realized I was covered with red ants that were biting me all over. By the time we got back, I had to be put into the tub and coated with baking soda. Grandma yelled at Grandpa, but he protested that he had told me not to, as he grinned to himself.

My birthday was in November, so I was going to have to wait another year to start school, but Sunday school teachers told my parents I was bright and shouldn't wait, so they decided to send me to the Catholic school in town. In order to do that, as a five-year-old, I had to catch a Greyhound bus every morning as it passed on the highway running by the inn, ride 10 miles into town, then walk through heavy downtown traffic two miles to school, reversing the process after school. As soon as the snowbirds left, we moved back into town, etc.

My father's mother was bipolar. All summer she would work around the clock with unlimited energy running the inn, entertaining the guests with her bawdy jokes, and keeping everything running seamlessly. She had gorgeous flowers all over the grounds, including a bank of thrift (creeping phlox), a yard full of irises of all colors and a huge garden across the road of the most beautiful dahlias I've ever seen anywhere. They were every color and design of the rainbow and the size of dinner plates. People came from all over to buy a dozen dahlias, which was an armful. Then in the fall, my grandparents closed up the inn, dug up the dahlia bulbs to be preserved in the basement, and Grandma turned into a lunatic. She would go after Grandpa with a large piece of stove wood. He would run, but sometimes she connected and he would be badly injured. At times he would come stay with us for two or three weeks to protect himself. Grandma got it into her head that he had fathered my two sisters during some of these stays, and she wanted to kill all of them. I remember times when my mother would lock up the house and keep everyone inside, because Grandma had threatened to come with a rifle to kill them all, but she never did. I was considered to be the only legitimate grandchild, so she played Santa Claus for me, getting me whatever my parents told her to get, which was usually something they wanted, such as a pedal-wagon (tricycle with an attached wagon), which my mother wanted to help carry groceries, or a basketball and hoop for my father. She did get me a doll every year for my birthday until I was 12, at which time my mother took all my dolls and burned them. For my 12th birthday Grandma got me a 50-year old, upright mahogany piano and two music books that were published in 1895. She also paid for a year of piano lessons. The piano was and is still beautiful and the lessons were enough to allow me to play in church for many years. Grandma may have been crazy, but she helped instill in me a love of music and flowers that will last my whole life, and that helped me survive a really painful childhood.

As a postscript, after I was grown, my other Grandma told me that Grandma Elton was a known shop-lifter and had been banned from many stores in town, so many of the gifts she gave me were probably "hot".

CHAPTER FIVE

I was allowed to run wild most of my younger years. Ona never knew where I was and she didn't care. I'm sure she was hoping I wouldn't come back. As a result I had many exciting experiences that were actually quite dangerous. At the snowbird house, I made friends with a neighbor girl, Patty, who was two years older and allowed by an indulgent grandmother to do anything she wanted. Under her tutelage I learned to roller skate and it was mostly down the hill on the lawn of the nearby funeral home. They quite often told us to get off the grass, but we always came back. One day they left their garage door open and we went in to check out the hearses. They closed the door and we were suddenly in frightening darkness. After a few minutes they let us out and we ran like scared rabbits. I'm sure they had a good laugh and we learned our lesson. However, the courthouse was nearby and Patty wanted to see inside, so we walked the ledge all around the building peeking into windows. The courthouse was built on the side of a steep hill, so the ledge in the back was 20 feet off the ground. If we had slipped and fallen.....or if we had slipped and fallen into the pond where we often played..... I was an avid reader, so I regularly walked eight blocks to the library and came home carrying as many books as I could hold. At the age of six, I was reading classics like "Little Women", The Ancient Mariner", etc. My mother would give me money to pay utility bills and send me all over town to pay them. Patty and I walked miles to see school friends. Nobody cared.

My sister, Beth, was born when I was seven. She was colicky (later turned out to be bipolar) and difficult, so I was ignored. This all ended when I turned ten, and my sister, Janice, was born. Then it dawned on my mother that she had built-in slave labor. From then on, I raised my two sisters and did all the housework. Everything I did was criticized. I remember once I was accused of having stuck Janice with a pin when I changed her diaper, which I had not. I was sent to bed without supper. This was worse than a beating, because we were poor and food was really important. I remember being always hungry. School lunches were my salvation–the only place I ever got meat or milk. My health has always been problematic, and I'm sure early malnutrition has been a factor. I'm also told that my asthma is caused by my father's heavy smoking during all my formative years. I couldn't even count all the times I was dragged out of bed and sent walking in all kinds of weather to the store to buy cigarettes.

Please let it be enough.

CHAPTER SIX

Our church had a week-long convention in Bloomington, Indiana, every summer. A family friend took me on the bus across country the year I was 11. The next year I made the trip alone and the year after that I took my sister, Beth, with me. I'm sure my parents didn't pay for it.

Ona always sucked up to rich people and insisted that I have only rich friends. Once I was invited to a rich girl's birthday party and told to wear school clothes, so we could play outdoors. My mother bought a piece of brilliant magenta fabric and made a fancy dress. I argued, (I never wore dresses, preferring to live in jeans and a T-shirt) but had to wear the dress and walk two miles to her party, where everybody else was in school clothes and got to play while I watched, VERY embarrassed.

My father would make me play checkers with him, acting as though he was doing me a favor. He ALWAYS won, backing me into a corner. It happened so often, I started having a recurring dream of a very large room that had a checkerboard floor and no furniture. At the far end of the room was a large black cloud that was coming towards me, encompassing everything as it came. I would wake up with one leg out of the bed, trying to run.

When I was 10 and 11, we actually lived in one place for 3 ½ years. It was in the basement of the landlord's house. It had only one bedroom, so my sister, Beth, and I slept there, while my parents closed off the dining room and made it their bedroom, adding a crib for Janice later. The place was crawling with all sorts of bugs. There was a long, dark, scary hallway to walk down at night, and I would say over and over, "God is love—love casteth out fear", in order to get to my room at night. When I turned on the light, the walls appeared to be alive with movement of all the insects, running for cover.

I had two main chores every day. One was to fill a can with kerosene at the barrel outside and empty it into the stove indoors. The other was to wash the baby's diapers by hand in the bathtub. We had no hot water, so it had to be heated on the stove, as I did when I washed dishes. I would have to make sure the diapers were perfectly clean and then go hang them outside on the clothes line. We took one bath a week when the little wood stove was operated to heat enough water for baths and laundry. I was expected to go out into the woods regularly to collect gunny sacks full of pine cones to make a fire with. We had a semi-automatic washing machine. A load of clothes would be put into hot water for a wash cycle. Then the clothes would be wrung out by hand and set aside. A second load of clothes would be placed into the same water. At the end of the cycle the water would drain out into a tub. I had to be ready with two five-gallon buckets to quickly scoop up the water and carry it outdoors, dump it in a ditch and run back in to scoop up more water, out again, until all the water was gone. Then the rinse would be started and I would have to go through the same process. Those buckets were really heavy for a little kid to handle, but I had no choice.

My teacher gave a hygiene lesson at school one day, stating that everyone should wash every day and put on clean clothes. I just knew she was talking to and about me. I wanted to melt into the floorboards, I was so embarrassed.

My mother insisted on green beans being cooked for hours, until they were gray mush. I thought I hated beans--what a delightful surprise years later to find out they could actually be eaten green! As hungry as I was, there came a day when I just couldn't choke them down. I was made to sit for hours, till I finally threw them on the floor behind the little wood stove. My mother found them and made me eat them off the floor.

I came home from school one day very hungry and spotted a bunch of bananas on top of the refrigerator. I didn't even like bananas, because my parents would force me to eat rotten ones, so they wouldn't have to feel guilty about throwing them away. I was really hungry and ate one, figuring they wouldn't miss it. However, they did, and ganged up on me, screaming in my face until I was hysterical and sending me to bed without supper.

The landlady watched my sisters while I was at school, but the rest of the time they were my responsibility at the age of 10. One day I was dancing around with Beth, when she ran into a floor lamp, knocked it over and broke it. I knew I was going to get a beating, so I thought fast. We had no phone, so I ran upstairs and used the landlady's phone to call my mother at work. I figured if I had witnesses, they couldn't punish me—it worked!

Where we lived was close to a golf course, just a path through a little patch of woods and there was "my tree" next to the golf course. I would often be up in the tree when a golfer would hit his ball into the little wooded area. I would holler out to tell him where the ball was, and it would scare him half to death, because a voice was coming out of the air. Some would grab their ball and run; others would just run, leaving their ball for me to take down to the little country store to be turned in for a candy bar. I had a good thing going.

An odd quirk to this story is that many years later I came back to see my old living quarters and walked out into the woods—there was the same path leading down to "my tree". I started to walk down the path and fell flat on my face. I tried it again with the same results. I was scratching my head, when it came to me: my brain was programmed to walk down that path as a 10-year-old. My brain was NOT programmed to walk down it as an adult—I was taller, legs were longer, etc. I walked alongside the path and was fine. Amazing how the brain works!

CHAPTER SEVEN

I was into all the sports at school, and was the second fastest runner in school. The fastest was Margaret Roper. One day a rumor was going around that Margaret had gotten in trouble with the principal and I was the one who had told on her, so she was going to get me after school. Margaret was the toughest, meanest kid in school—all the boys were afraid of her. I had not told on her, and had no idea what this was all about, but I knew it was useless to try to reason with her. I had to figure out how to survive. She could run faster than me, so I had to get a head start.

We were both walkers, but lived in different directions. I just had to outrun her till she gave up and had to go home. Our little community was called Valley Hill for a good reason. The school was built on a hill. The road ran down the hill, where it died into the main road; then the golf course was on the other side. When the bell rang I threw my books at a neighbor girl, went out the front door, rather than the required side door, and ran down that hill on loose gravel like my life depended on it—which it did. I could hear her footsteps hot behind me. School buses were passing by with kids hanging out the windows yelling. I was praying that there would be no traffic at the foot of the hill, and there wasn't. I ran straight across onto the golf course, across the little bridge and up the long hill. Halfway up the hill she collapsed, and said, "I'll get you tomorrow", and went home. I, of course, did not tell my parents and we didn't have a phone. I went to school the next day fearfully, but the principal had straightened Margaret out and she had to get up in front of the class and apologize, along with her father, in order to get back in school.

CHAPTER EIGHT

When I was around 12, we moved to a very different area from what I was used to. I was very athletic, played softball, did gymnastics, and prided myself on my ability to climb any tree. The neighbor kids dared me to climb a certain tree, so, of course, I had to do it. Unbeknownst to me, it was a sycamore tree, unfamiliar to me. Sycamores shed all of their bark once a year, in a solid sheath. I had climbed far up into the tree, when all the bark came off in my arms, and I fell backwards, hitting each branch as I went down. I landed on the ground on my back, knocking myself out as I heard the neighbor kids running away laughing. I have had back problems all my life ever since, but I never told my parents—I learned early on never to talk to them any more than necessary, because they would turn it around to be my fault, and I would get a beating. I don't remember ever getting a kind word from either parent, but they made fun of me often. They delighted in giving me a job to do, refusing to tell me how to do it, then beating me for doing it wrong.

I was invited for a weekend to the home of a rich girl I barely knew and didn't like, but my mother made me go. When

I got there, I found the whole family was sick, and I really should not have gone. I stuck it out, but came home sick myself. At first it appeared to be just a cold, but it continued to get worse, till finally I was taken to the doctor. He examined me and then very dramatically walked over to the phone and reserved a room for me at the hospital. Only then did he inform us that I had lobar pneumonia. In those days penicillin was new and in injection form only, so I was in the hospital for a week getting three shots a day in my derriere. I also had to take sulfur capsules, which were too large for me to swallow, so they were emptied into a tablespoon with a little Karo syrup and I had to swallow that six times a day. I was put on a soft diet, which consisted of one soft-boiled egg, cream of mushroom soup and green Jello. All because my mother had to kiss up to rich people.

The neighbors came to visit and brought me a bag of Easter candy eggs. My mother took them home, saying I would get them back once I was allowed to eat. I never saw them again. I had nothing else to do, so I wrote a poem:

> "When you are in the hospital, you can get bored,
> Unless into you a hole is bored.
> The penicillin will hurt for a while,
> But after that you can stop and smile,
> And say. 'Oh, it was nothing at all',
> As you feel of that hole, even though it's small.
> You've got a few pastimes--they're not very big,
> And they've got you on a diet,
> When you could eat a pig.

The flowers are very pretty and gay,
But you can't forget that you're going to get three shots
a day."

A dog, a white Spitz, wandered into our yard and became my dog. He had perky brown ears, so he became Perky. One day I had had a bad beating and was sitting on the steps crying. All of a sudden there was Perky with his head on my lap and sympathetic tears in his eyes. Finally, somebody cared. Soon after, I walked out to the road to go to school and there was Perky, dead in the middle of the busy highway. I was inconsolable, crying my eyes out. My mother made me go to school with a red, puffy face—she didn't care. At school some mean boys had seen Perky's body in the road, and they laughed and made fun of my grief. I didn't think I would ever get through that day or many thereafter—I had lost my best friend—forever.

Please let it be enough.

CHAPTER NINE

I always remember my three worse beatings. One was the one previously mentioned with the broom handle. The second involved our garden. Wherever we lived at the time, my father would have the garden area plowed, my mother would sow the seeds, and then the rest of the season the garden was my responsibility–I did all the hoeing, weeding, harvesting, and I even learned to use the big pressure cooker for canning. I remember one year my father impulsively bought several very ripe bushels of peaches off a truck at the side of the road, and it was left to me to peel, slice and can them–47 quarts. I remember the number because we used the type of Ball jar that had lids that popped as they sealed. I had to count the pops. Anyway, this one year Ona had planted lots and lots of leaf lettuce, which does not grow in a head, but individually. They are covered with dirt and require being put through at least three washings of a large tub full of lettuce. Once they are clean, they are put into a large pot and slowly cooked down–wilted–until they can be made into a salad with oil and vinegar. The process of picking, washing and cooking takes between two and three hours. My parents had a business school at the time and would come home for lunch. I had instructions to have a "mess" of lettuce ready for lunch every day. One day I lost track of the time, having the care of my sisters and other housework to do. By the time I realized it, there wasn't enough time to get it done. When they got home and had no lettuce for lunch, my father went outside and cut a branch off a small tree, came in and beat me mercilessly with it. I had large bloody welts all over my legs, but the worst was on my heels. We tend to think of heels as being tough, but actually they are quite tender. I could barely walk and was in acute pain the rest of the summer. It was well that I went barefoot all summer, as I would never have been able to wear shoes. No medication was offered.

The third worst beating involved a bolo paddle. These days a bolo paddle is made of light balsa wood, but back then it was quite thick and heavy, and capable of being used as a weapon. I have no idea what my supposed crime was, but my father forced me to remove all my clothes. He then hit me as hard as he could on my bare buttocks, going back and forth from one side to the other. I tried my best not to flinch, but eventually he hit a nerve on the right side and I couldn't help it. As soon as he saw the flinch, he concentrated on that side till I was in absolute agony. I have had to deal with pain from that nerve ever since and have actually had to have major surgery to repair it.

Please let it be enough.

CHAPTER TEN

When I reached puberty and showed physical signs of growing up, I became more attractive to Carter. Ona had mixed reactions to this. On the one hand she was happy he was paying less attention to her, but on the other hand she was jealous. The insulting remarks increased. I remember her calling me "fat" when I weighed 120 pounds. She refused to buy me any underwear, and forced me to wear her old, stretched out underwear, folded over with large safety pins. This was immensely embarrassing having to get undressed in front of the other girls in four years of gym class and basketball practice.

Please let it be enough.

CHAPTER ELEVEN

When I was 15, Ona's family decided Carter was the cause of all the problems in our family, so they engineered a fast pack-up and escape to the home of Ona's sister in Tennessee. Ona told me she had packed all my things, but much later I found that she had left my few personal belongings behind, never to be seen again. In Tennessee I felt like I had been transported to heaven. I was given one small chore a day and then I was FREE! They had no idea the hell I had been living through. The first day I just sat in the living room afraid to move. I had never been allowed to walk from one room to another without permission. Hour by hour I got bolder and bolder until finally I actually walked outside! And nobody yelled at me or gave me a beating! Unbelievable! I had no idea what to do with myself with all this free time. So my uncle told me I could ride my cousin's bike. He had no idea that I had never been on a bike and didn't know how to ride. So, I taught myself how to ride and the next day asked for permission to go out of the yard. I was told I could go anywhere I wanted to. They lived way out in the country on a hill, so I learned to ride down hills (don't do it with your mouth open, unless you like bugs for lunch), and pump up hills. Then came the day when my father came to visit. He was not allowed on the property, so I was to take my little sisters out to the edge of the road with strict instructions not to go out into the road or he could take us. I followed instructions until Carter tried to grab us and drag us into the road. I was caught in a struggle while my uncle and cousins came running carrying a pitchfork.

All went well until one day we were all scattered far and wide, when my aunt rang her cowbell vigorously, which was the signal for everybody to come running home. We all assumed there was an emergency, but then we saw a large watermelon sitting on the picnic table in the back yard. My sisters and I gagged and ran away, refusing to eat any. My aunt was very insulted. She had no idea what we had gone through the previous summer. My father had read a book claiming that watermelon was the perfect food, so we had had to live on watermelon the entire summer. We never wanted to see a watermelon for the rest of our lives. Another summer he read that peanuts were the perfect food, so we had multiple rows of peanuts in our garden, that I had to hoe, weed and harvest. Then he read another book that said peanuts are poisonous, so all those peanuts just sat there and molded till they were eventually thrown out.

I got to go to 4-H camp, had a boyfriend, and started school in the fall. The family plan was for Ona to get a job, then an apartment and move her three daughters there with her. She got a job, but when it came close to time to follow through on the rest, all of a sudden she had to go back home to sign some papers with her lawyer. She was barely gone when I got a postcard from her telling me to pack up all our things and be ready for her to come pick us up and move back home. I was devastated, refused to go, and went and hid out down by the creek I loved so well. My uncle found me and said legally there was nothing they could do—I had to go. Ona came and got us after a lot of yelling between her and my aunt and uncle. She promised that Carter would not be living with us. We were barely in the door, when Carter appeared holding ten records. He said he had gone to the record store and asked for the ten top records—all I had to do was accept him back and the records were mine. I wanted those records with all my heart and being—nobody ever gave me anything—but I had to say, no. Ona slapped me hard across the face and screamed, "You are trying to ruin my life!" My sister, Beth, was only 8 at the time, but 40 years later she repeated that scene to Ona, who flatly denied it.

CHAPTER TWELVE

My high school years were total torture with school itself being my only solace. My principal stepped in several times to help me. One day I badly sprained my foot at basketball practice. Mr. Jasper regularly gave me rides to and from practice and games–my parents never once attended any of my games or anything else. My foot was hurt badly, so I missed school the next day. I had perfect attendance, and we had no phone, so Mr. Jasper came to my house, took one look at my foot and left. An hour later my mother came flying grimly through the door and ordered me to get up to go to the doctor. The doctor X-rayed my foot twice, because he couldn't believe it wasn't broken. I have no idea who paid the medical expenses, but I have no doubt that Mr. Jasper got me to the doctor. The next year the Beta Club was going to the state capital for the weekend, but my parents said, no. Somehow or other, the night before, Ona told me to pack to go. The same thing happened for the Senior trip. I also got a little assistance from my Uncle Lewen, when we lived next door for a while. He was a wonderful husband and father and very hard worker with a great sense of humor. His one way of relaxing was fishing. He knew I was having a hard time, so he offered to pay me $1.00 for a dozen night-crawlers, which was way above the usual price. I hated going out at night and crawling around in wet grass to catch the slimey, disgusting worms, but a dollar was a huge sum of money when I never got a penny any other way.

Life resumed as before, which was the way Ona wanted it. Carter was her own private pit bull. She liked being able to sic him on people she didn't like and use him as an excuse to avoid doing things she didn't want to do. Without him, she had no excuse for her own behavior. She also needed me back to do all her work for her. It was only years later when I was finally able to go to college at age 36 and studied abnormal psychology, that I realized she was a sociopath, manipulating and lying her way through life.

Please let it be enough.

CHAPTER THIRTEEN

Our high school participated in an academic competition every year, which was held on a college campus a three-hour drive away. The principal chose one person per subject to represent the school, and we all rode together on a school bus to take tests in our individual subjects. As a freshman I had a science project, which did not win. As a sophomore I was to compete in English grammar, but our bus had mechanical problems and we arrived after the tests had already started. It took a lot of arguing, but the registrar finally allowed us in, but in the rush of registering, she accidentally sent me to English lit. By the time I realized the error, it was too late to do anything about it. I could have aced the grammar test, but knew little about lit, so did poorly. As a junior I was sent in math. I placed third and would have gotten an award, but there was a tie for second and they took only the top three. I did, however, meet the young man who was first, Jerry, and we were attracted to each other. We talked quite a while. I found out he was very religious, and planned to be both a doctor and a missionary in China. We exchanged addresses and wrote back and forth at least weekly. I was dreaming of joining him in China. As a senior I went to the competition in writing composition. When I entered the testing room, I recognized a girl who attended a neighboring school and had been written up in our newspaper as a promising journalism major. I knew she would probably win, and when I saw that our topic was to be "Television", I realized I could not write a serious paper, since I had never had a TV. My only hope was to go for a comedic satire, based on the criticisms of others. At the award ceremony none of the representatives of our school were winning as they usually did—gloom and doom settled over our group. When we finally got to the writing section, the journalism girl, of course, won, but then I heard my name being read out in second place. A cheer went up--I was the only one who won an award that year—I was the hero! I saw little of Jerry, but we were still on.

I was eagerly awaiting being able to go to college, but my parents refused to allow me to go, and I was only 17 when I graduated from high school, so I could not leave till I was 18. By then I had a job and my main ambition was just to get out of that house. My only regret at leaving was the fear that the abuse would then be passed on to my little sisters. Unfortunately, it was passed on to Beth. Many years later she made Carter sit down and listen to a recitation of every-thing he had done to her. He listened quietly and then went into the bathroom for 20 minutes. When he came out, he said he had always wondered why his daughters hated him, but he had no memory of any of it.

He had also attacked Janice, but she's a scrapper. She fought back and actually punched him. Then she went out the window and stayed several days with a friend.

My father had said I couldn't go to college because it was "the place of the devil". Years later when I was finally able to go, he made remarks about how college didn't mean anything, because all he had to do was take a test and he could get a diploma. That's when I figured out that he was just jealous and didn't want me to do something that he hadn't done.

Please let it be enough.

CHAPTER FOURTEEN

When I was in Tennessee, my aunt had given me a diary, which I had never had before, but I soon found it to be a good outlet for emotions. When we went back to live with Carter, we moved to a house where for the first time in my life, I had a room of my own. That was nice, but it made it easier for Carter to assault me with no witnesses. I hid my diary between my bureau and the wall. I was invited to a birthday party of a rich boy that I barely knew. It was to be held in the evening at a summer camp in the woods. I did not want to go, but my mother knew the parents and insisted. In the afternoon we were given a tour of the camp. We stopped to watch some kids swinging out on a rope over a small lake, where they let go and went swimming. One girl was afraid to try, but the others talked her into it. She swung out, changed her mind and let go too late, landing hard on the ground. As she lay there, not moving, our guide hustled us away, saying she would be fine. I will never forget that girl and will always wonder just how all right she really was.

The party involved dancing, which I didn't know how to do, so I was happy to finally leave. As I walked into our house,

I discovered my father reading my diary. He delightedly threw all my personal and private writings into my face, making fun of it all, especially anything about Jerry. This was particularly painful, because Jerry had suddenly stopped writing and hadn't answered any of my letters for the last month. This mocking went on for weeks.

At Christmas my father decided to take a trip to Florida to go deep sea fishing. He wanted Beth to go with him. Then my mother decided that Beth was too young to go without supervision, so I had to go, too. I did not want to go and was looking forward to being without Carter for a few days, but since when did anyone care what I thought? Carter drove somewhere down on the east coast of Florida and got a motel room. The next morning he left to go fishing and told me to go out on the beach with Beth. I had no idea where the beach was, but I walked a ways and saw the ocean, so I got Beth settled with her little pail and shovel in the sand and looked around, bored. There was no one on the beach and a red flag was blowing in the wind. I had no way of knowing that the red flag was a warning of bad weather and that was why no one was there. I also had no way of knowing that we were on the ocean side of a barrier island, when we should have been on the quiet, peaceful inner side away from the wind and waves. Innocently and ignorantly, I idly thought I should at least wade in the water to be able to say I had been in the Atlantic Ocean. I waded in up to my knees, when I was suddenly swept away by the undertow. Before I could take a breath, I was being rolled over and over in a mixture of salt water and sand, totally out of control. It was extremely frightening as I fought to get to my feet and breathe some air. This felt like it went on for an eternity and I was running out of strength, fearing death. Suddenly my hand closed around a cable and I pulled myself hand over hand onto the beach, where I lay gasping for air. When I was able to get to my feet, I looked for my sister, and panicked when I did not see her. I thought I had lost my little sister. Finally, way far up the beach, I saw a small speck, and ran toward it. There was Beth still happily digging in the sand, totally unaware that I had even been gone. There is no doubt in my mind that my guardian angel put that cable in my hand. Otherwise I would have been dead. When I told my father what had happened, he yelled at me for being so stupid as to go to the wrong side of the island. The next day we went to the right side of the island, where Beth went back to her pail and shovel, while I lay down on my stomach on the sand and went to sleep. I woke up with the worst sunburn I have ever had. I was in a lot of pain and needed medical attention, but my father just yelled at me again for being stupid. The next day he decided to drive down to Miami, just so he could say he had been to Miami. I was in no condition to go, so I stayed in bed. The next day we headed for home. As we started up the mountain, it began to snow heavily. Halfway up the mountain, the car in front of us suddenly spun around and around and went off the road coming to rest in some bushes hanging over a creek. I told my father to stop—we had to help them. He just kept going. I still see that car in my mind wondering what condition they were in and what we could and should have done.

CHAPTER FIFTEEN

When I was 15, I met a 17-year-old boy named Neddie. His father was a carpenter foreman for a large construction company that was building a Gerber plant nearby, and Neddie had gotten a summer job with them. The two of them had rented a room nearby and went home to S.C. on weekends. I met Neddie through a neighbor and we started spending as much time together as possible. I, of course, was not allowed to date. The only reason my father accepted Neddie was that they both liked to fish, so my father spent more time with Neddie than I did. I came to really resent fishing and begged to go with them. Eventually they relented and I went. I was able to cast my line further than either of them, but nothing was biting and it started to rain, so I spent a very boring evening sitting alone in the truck and that was the end of my fishing experience. At the end of the summer, Neddie and his father went home and I thought I would never see him again.

When I graduated from high school, my parents made me attend their business school. I had learned to type in high school and then added on shorthand. I got a job in a small manufacturing firm working for the husband of my high school typing teacher. I also left home and got my own little apartment. One night I unexpectedly got a call from Neddie, inviting me to accompany the family on a road trip to his brother's wedding in Little Rock. So, I went, scrunched six in the car, driving all night, getting there in time to change clothes, attend the wedding, change clothes again, and then back into the car for the overnight return trip. About all I remember about the trip was the bridge over the Mississippi River and how bad the Alabama roads were. I kept dozing off and waking up just in time to keep Neddie from running off the road. I got home barely in time to shower, dress and go to work. I actually went to sleep while typing a letter and fell off my chair into the floor. A kind fellow worker allowed me to sleep several hours in her car.

The next time I heard from Neddie, I was invited to come visit him at his home in S.C. I went and stayed at his parents' house. This turned out to be an unbelievable experience. I had grown up poor and had lived in many rundown places, but nothing prepared me for what I was about to see. Neddie's wooden home was barely holding together, had never had a coat of paint, with no underpinning and the kitchen had a hole in the floor three feet across. When they swept, the dirt just went out the hole.

I had my own room. The next morning I was awakened by Neddie's father, who was falling-down drunk, pawing at me and trying to crawl into bed with me. After a few minutes of my fighting him, several family members arrived and removed him. I was to learn that Neddie's father stayed sober all week and did his job well, but then came home and stayed roaring drunk all weekend. I watched as they all played catch, throwing his car keys around to keep them away from him.

Neddie wanted me to meet his grandmother, so we went to her house. It is difficult to describe the experience and do it justice. Her house was in the swamp. It was so badly neglected that it was sinking down into the swamp and becoming a part of it. Walking up onto the porch was hazardous because of all the collapsing boards. Inside were upholstered chairs that had obviously not been sat in for many years, wet and filthy. I didn't want to touch anything and couldn't get out of there fast enough. At no point was Neddie the least bit apologetic. He obviously was accustomed to all this—it was his way of life.

Now you would think that I would want to get as far away from all this as possible, but that is because you don't understand the psyche of an abused and neglected child. He had the most beautiful clear gray eyes and long lashes I had ever seen. Neddie asked me to marry him and said those magic words that I so badly needed to hear, "I love you". Nobody had ever said those words to me, so I accepted. We went to a justice of the peace and filled out the paperwork, but they required a week to be legal, so Neddie drove me all the way back home, where I gave notice at work and packed up my belongings. The next weekend he came for me, we drove back to S.C., were married, had a one-night honeymoon at a friend's house, and moved into a rental house.

Neddie had a job as a butcher at the local Piggly Wiggly store and I looked for work. All I could find was running the register at Piggly Wiggly with no paycheck—just a few groceries. There I became acquainted with the plight of the black population. They gathered outside at the end of the day to go through whatever garbage the store threw out. As I learned more about the local hierarchy, I felt as though I had stepped into a scene from "To Kill a Mockingbird". The black women looked for jobs in the white households as housekeepers, cooks and nannies for the white children. They were sometimes allowed to take home discarded clothing and the leftovers from the white owners' plates. The black men rarely got work, just occasionally if the white family needed yard work or heavy lifting. I will never forget one day at the store when an elderly black lady came through my register with a pitifully small amount of groceries. She was short two cents and had to decide what to put back. It was a difficult decision and she agonized over it, causing the white woman behind her with a cart piled full of food, to become quite annoyed. I was torn between crying because I didn't have the two cents to give her, and an overwhelming urge to punch out that self-centered woman behind her who could have very easily paid the two cents, but didn't care. How ironic that those white women despised the blacks and yet were willing to give over the care of their most precious possessions—their children—to them.

I eventually found a temporary receptionist job at a carpet company, but it was in the next town. I didn't have a driver's license and Neddie's prize possession was his brand-new Chevy, which he wouldn't let me anywhere near, so a friend offered to drive me to and from work, since he also worked there. Bubba also helped me get my driver's license. My job was for six weeks only. At the end of the six weeks, Bubba said he had to put in overtime and let me drive his car home. I was barely home and in my bedroom changing clothes, when Bubba suddenly burst into the house, grabbed me, started pulling off my clothes and kissing me. I fought him off, and found him to be indignant. He figured he had done all those favors for me, so I owed him. His wife was pregnant at the time and had refused him any intimacy, so he expected me to make up for it. I figured it was a one-time event and let it go. A week later I was in the kitchen ironing, when Bubba abruptly appeared again—this time determined to get what he wanted. Thank God I had a hot iron in my hands and was able to back into a corner and hold him off. From then on, the doors were kept locked. I never told Neddie, because I knew he had a gun in the house that he used to kill water moccasins when he went fishing in the swamps. I wasn't sure whether he would feel he had to go after Bubba or not.

In the meantime Neddie's brother came home from the army on leave. We had a second bedroom, so he stayed with us. Harry was home all day with me. We talked, played cards and watched TV. I innocently thought that was all there was to it. Then came the day when I was making his bed—Harry ran in, threw me on the bed, pinned me down and started kissing me. I fought as hard as I could and got away. Again, he thought I owed him. I was so relieved when his leave was over.

Please let it be enough.

CHAPTER SIXTEEN

I had made friends with some neighbors, a young couple with a baby. Neddie told me repeatedly to stay away from them. I asked for an explanation several times before he finally said they were black. They were blonde with a tow-headed baby, so I had no idea what he was talking about. He explained that ten generations back there had been a black person in their heritage, so that made them black. I was flabbergasted and continued to see them. They invited us for dinner. It took a lot of arguing, but I eventually talked Neddie into going. As we were sitting at the table trying to make conversation, a man appeared at the door saying he had been trying to reach Neddie to tell him his father and grandmother had been in a serious car accident. Neddie was extremely angry with me for being caught at a black family's house, and for making it difficult to reach him with the news. We raced to the hospital and were told that his father had a broken arm and his elderly, overweight grandmother had a broken hip. She had to go live with Neddie's uncle, because she couldn't care for herself, which left her "house" vacant. It seems that Neddie's father had been left home alone, drunk as usual, and he had decided he wanted his mother to make him some soup, so he drove to go get her. On the way home he made a left turn in front of a speeding convertible carrying four teenagers home from college. The four kids were seriously injured and not expected to live. Neddie had friends in the local police department, so, of course, no charges were made.

We had been married six months when Neddie's cousin and aunt came to town for a visit. His cousin was what we used to call a "floozy". She had bleached blonde hair, thick make-up and absolutely no morals. She set out to get Neddie and succeeded. She climbed onto his lap and kissed him in my presence. When he didn't come home that night, I knew it was over. When he finally came home, he demanded that we move into his grandmother's vacant "house". That did it. I had no reason to continue living. The only money I had was some change in an old piggy bank. I got it out, walked into town and bought a bottle of aspirin. I swallowed as many aspirin as I could get down, then lay down on the couch, dramatically crossed my arms over my chest, and waited to die. Shortly thereafter, my sister-in-law arrived, telling me I had to go to a farewell party they were giving for the cousin. I didn't want to go, but she dragged me up, got me changed into dressier clothes and took me to their uncle's house. By then I wasn't feeling too well and went looking for a bed to lie down on. Laura followed me, demanded to know what was wrong and I told her what I had done. Laura got Neddie, who angrily took me to the doctor. He tried to pump my stomach. When I refused, he made me drink salt water, which caused me to repeatedly throw up. Then Neddie drove me to the hospital 26 miles away, yelling at me all the way. I just wanted to go to sleep, so they laid me across a very small cart where I was hanging off both sides and couldn't possibly go to sleep. I was in the hospital four days. A psychiatrist would occasionally come in and I would always pretend to be asleep. Somebody called my mother, who arrived angrily telling me how much I was embarrassing her and causing her to lose work. She lied to the doctors saying I was going to live with my Grandma Duncan. En route back, she told me Grandma had refused to take me because "she might try it again". So, I was right back again with my parents and their abuse.

Please let it be enough.

CHAPTER SEVENTEEN

I went into a deep depression, crying all day and listening to sad songs on the radio all night. I was sent to our church convention, but I just looked for somebody to listen to my sad story. Neddie got a divorce. My mother had finally found a steady job at a large corporation, so she eventually got me a temp job in the office where she worked. One temp job led to another and another, and I eventually got a permanent job in the Sales Department. My boss was a kindly middle-aged man who became like a father to me.

I loved to sing and joined a local choral group. One evening I was about to leave to go to practice for a concert; I was wearing a brand new lavender embroidered blouse that I really liked. My father started yelling at me that I couldn't go. He ripped off my blouse, shredding it beyond repair. Not wanting to lose any more blouses, I had to stay home.

I was constantly told that nothing belonged to me, not even the clothes on my back. Fairly often I would be thrown out of the house and be forced to sit all night on the steps outside, with no coat, regardless of the weather. At daybreak my mother would open the door and yell at me for sitting there all night—as if it was my decision. Then she would tell me to get inside before the neighbors saw me.

When I got out on my own again, I carried emotional scars that went deep. In my own apartment, I had a dream one night that I heard my father kill my mother right in my own living room. There was a pause. Then I heard his footsteps coming slowly toward my bedroom and I knew I was next. I awoke in a panic, half out of my bed. I was so scared, I couldn't move for hours, watching my bedroom door. Finally, slowly, slowly, I got myself back in bed, slid to a sitting position and reached up to turn on the little lamp over my bed. I stayed that way the rest of the night. It was months before I could sleep without the light on.

Please let it be enough.

CHAPTER EIGHTEEN

After a couple of years I went back to our convention, where I met a divorced man, Sam, with three children living with their mother. He was 19 years older than I was. He told me a sad story about his terrible ex-wife and I fell for it. We had a long-distance courtship, during which he wrote beautiful letters, which he later told me were copied out of books. He proposed and said those magical words, "I love you". He drove down to get me, we went over the state line where one-day paperwork was legal, and got married, moving back to his home state into an apartment.

I got pregnant immediately. When I was about six months along, Sam told me about all his girlfriends. What was I going to do? I didn't have a penny to my name, was not allowed a credit card or checkbook, and I certainly didn't have any family to go to. I was stuck. He had a cushy job that allowed him to goof off 95% of the time. I never knew where he was and neither did his boss. He was fired from several jobs for being drunk. I was given strict instructions never to use the phone, which effectively cut me off from the world.

Soon after Sam's admission, he decided we were going to go spend a weekend on a popular tourist island off the coast of Rhode Island. I was very pregnant and didn't feel like making such a trip, but I was not consulted. We stayed at a nice seaside hotel where the sound of the waves was soothing. During the night I had an attack of indigestion. My husband threw me out of bed for daring to disturb his sleep, and made me walk up and down the hall all night. We overheard a conversation between two old ladies that the east side of the island reminded them of the White Cliffs of Dover because of the high bluffs overlooking the ocean. Sam decided we were going for a walk and the hotel keeper warned us to stay on the road because the fog would be coming in. We walked a while till Sam spotted a path going off to the left and told me to go on it. I didn't want to after the warning we had received, but he shoved me onto it and made me walk ahead. Heavy fog moved in as we walked and I couldn't even see the path. I heard a roaring sound and stopped to listen. As I stopped, I looked down and suddenly realized I was standing on the edge of a cliff with roaring waves beneath. One more step and I would have fallen to my death, which is what Sam had hoped would happen. I turned around and ran.

Please let it be enough.

CHAPTER NINETEEN

As time went on, I realized my husband was a sociopath, just like my mother had been. When I later studied psychology and became a special education teacher, I marveled at how mistreated people will continue to make the same bad decisions, putting themselves back into harmful conditions over and over, which doesn't make any sense to others. They do it because that mistreatment is all they have ever known—it's familiar—they know exactly what their role is and what to expect. They feel out of place in safer surroundings and don't know how to act or respond.

On one occasion, our older son had had hernia surgery at the age of two. Sam had gotten reimbursed for the surgery twice from his job—once from work and again through the union. Yet he went to various ones at church and begged for money, pretending to be broke—he was an accomplished con man. He had met an elderly lady at a convention, who lived in New York City. She was quite poor and lived from one Social Security check to the next. Sam decided to go after her. He got an elderly friend to babysit and informed me that I was going with him to New York, which involved going on the train and then the subway. I had grown up in the country, had no experience with subways, did not know anything about the big city, and was very apprehensive about going. I asked questions, but Sam refused to explain where and how we were going. When we got to the subway, we were waiting on the platform when a train pulled up. I asked if this was our train and he said, no, so I relaxed and turned to look around. When I turned back, Sam was gone. I frantically looked around and saw that he had gotten on the train and the doors were starting to close. I jumped to the nearest door and pulled on it enough to be able to get in. I ran to the next car where Sam was. He just stood there coldly and never said a word. He had planned on just going off and leaving me there alone, totally lost with no money, no phone, to—what? Just die? When we finally got to the lady's apartment, he started begging for money. She, of course, had none, but he wasn't about to leave empty-handed. He spotted a large jar in which she had a little change. He stole that jar and triumphantly carried it all the way home on the subway and train.

Every night after supper the children would be excused to go play, but I would be expected to sit at the table for up to three hours and listen to a drunken tirade during which Sam would threaten to kill me. At the time I had long hair in a ponytail. If I ever tried to get up, Sam would grab my ponytail and swing me back into the chair.

Please let it be enough.

CHAPTER TWENTY

After 14 years of marriage and three children, ironically a rich "friend" that Sam was trying to get money out of, recommended a marriage counselor, who helped me grow enough of a backbone to make the decision to leave Sam. When I told him, he at first was extra nice to me to try to talk me out of it, but then reverted to his usual drunken mean self. I knew I had to get a job, but was concerned that my skills might have deteriorated, so I went out on temp jobs for a while. I quickly became the top temp at several agencies, but then all of a sudden I wasn't getting calls. I checked in with them and got run-around responses until finally one lady got up her nerve and said my husband had come to their agency and threatened them with bodily harm if they gave me any more work. Apparently he had done the same to others. By the grace of God I then got a permanent job from a newspaper ad and was going to work every day.

One of my regular chores at home was writing out checks to pay the bills. Sam would lay out the check book and the bills on his desk in the basement, where I was expected to fill them out before going to work. One day he told me to go do it, waited till I got to the head of the stairs and gave me a hard shove down the stairs. Fortunately, I had started to close the door so he shoved me at an angle sideways. I hit the partial wall on the left and ricocheted back to the right where I was able to catch hold of the railing and break my fall as I went down. I was also wearing a long robe, which helped to cushion my landing on the floor. Lying there I looked back up the stairs to see Sam standing there with the same cold stare he had had on the subway, just checking to see whether or not I was dead.

Please let it be enough.

One day Sam became angry when we were in the kitchen. He picked up a heavy wooden cutting board and started to hit me over the head. I ran, but he was between me and the door, so I had to run toward the back of the house. I went into our little half-bath and locked the door. He broke down the door, grabbed me around the neck and slammed me repeatedly against the towel rack, which broke. Then he started choking me. He worked out with weights every day and was very strong. I thought fast and realized if the police found me choked to death in my own home, they would know he was guilty, and he wouldn't want that to happen, so I went limp and played dead—he let go. I then wrote a codicil to my will, which stated that if my husband murdered me and was in jail, my three children were to go into the custody of my best friends. I made several copies and handed them out sealed to friends.

Please let it be enough.

Sam took my car away once he knew I needed transportation, so a friend helped me get a little Vega. It was a gas and oil guzzler, but it got me back and forth. I found an apartment in another town and decided one day to take a few items to my new apartment and take my daughter along to see her new home. When Sam saw us in the car, he was furious. He came running out and started rocking the car back and forth trying to turn it over. As I said, he was very strong and there was no doubt in my mind that he could do it. At first we just hung on till it dawned on me that I needed to start the engine and when the wheels touched the ground I could get out of there. Once I did, I flew down the road, fearing he would follow. Once I was sure he wasn't, I pulled over to catch my breath. My daughter asked, "Mommy, is Daddy going to kill you?"

Please let it be enough.

I couldn't afford a lawyer, so I used the services of a women's organization. Sam got a lawyer of the type that crawls out from under a rock. The first time we went to court I just wanted to be allowed to take my children into our new apartment. Instead the judge said I should keep the house, and ordered Sam to get out. We came home and I said to Sam, "We should sit the children down and explain what is going on." He agreed. We went into the living room with the children, where he abruptly grabbed me and started trying to drag me to the bedroom. His snake of a lawyer had told him if we had sex, the hearing would be null and void. My nerves were at a breaking point. I grabbed hold of the arm of the couch and held on for dear life while crying and screaming. It was a terrible scene to have in front of the children, but it worked—he finally let go. I went and called my lawyer, because Sam was saying that the judge hadn't meant for him to get out right away—he could have all the time he needed to find a new place to live, which meant never. My lawyer called his lawyer, who called Sam and told him he had to get out immediately.

I had decided for religious reasons to get a separation rather than a divorce. When we got to court for the second hearing, I was prepared with several witnesses: a bank manager to prove that Sam had lied on his financial statement, a real estate man to prove he had lied about the value of the house, a court social worker to state that her examination recommended Sam cared only for himself so the kids should go to my custody, etc. We walked in and heard the judge say he was not interested in hearing our case; we were to go out and make an agreement on our own, come back with it and he would sign it. Obviously, he had been paid off. So, my lawyer and I went to one coffee house and Sam and his lawyer went to another. Messengers were sent back and forth. First of all, Sam said he wanted custody, which was a lie, but in order to get custody I had to give up alimony and agree to $42 a week for child support—a teenager can eat that much in one day. I also had to settle for $25,000 from a house that ultimately sold for $185,000, and even that was to be divided up into two years.

I made two bad choices in marriage and there is no doubt in my mind that my childhood experiences played a large role in those bad choices. I was accustomed to being a victim and continued to be so.

Please let it be enough.

CHAPTER TWENTY-ONE

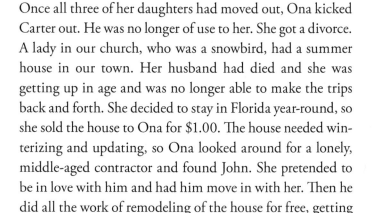

Once all three of her daughters had moved out, Ona kicked Carter out. He was no longer of use to her. She got a divorce. A lady in our church, who was a snowbird, had a summer house in our town. Her husband had died and she was getting up in age and was no longer able to make the trips back and forth. She decided to stay in Florida year-round, so she sold the house to Ona for $1.00. The house needed winterizing and updating, so Ona looked around for a lonely, middle-aged contractor and found John. She pretended to be in love with him and had him move in with her. Then he did all the work of remodeling of the house for free, getting wholesale prices on materials. Once the work was done, she kicked him out, knowing full well that he had a heart condition. He had to live in a small, rented room until he had a heart attack and died.

My father also had a heart condition from all his years of smoking. He died of a heart attack in 1989, right after I returned from a trip to Israel and Egypt. My last contact with him was an angry phone call wanting to know why I had not sent him any postcards from my trip. I told him I had sent him two cards, but he insisted that he had never gotten them. A week later he was dead. My mother and I cleaned out his belongings to get his mobile home ready to be sold, and there on his desk was one of the cards I had sent him.

My mother called me when Carter died and said I had to come home for the funeral. I didn't want to go, but she explained that Carter had not had a will, the two of them had been divorced, so I, as the oldest child, had to legally take charge. The hospital wouldn't even release the body to the funeral home without my okay. I called my sister Janice in California and told her, "If I've got to go, then so do you." We both reluctantly went. There was no funeral service, because Carter had no friends. When it came time for the family viewing, Ona insisted on our entering the room formally, with her on my arm and my sisters trailing behind. We all laughed, because there was no one there to see how we walked in. She angrily asked us why we had even bothered to come. Without forethought, Janice and I replied in unison, "Because we had to make sure he was really dead."

My sister wrote me that she had just had an eye appointment with Dr. Jerry Tobin and he had asked her about me. After all those years, we got in touch again. Unfortunately, he had inherited a kidney disease from his father, which had caused a stroke and paralysis of his left side. He had gotten his medical degree in the navy and had worked in Africa, rather than China, but otherwise had fulfilled his dream and had become an expert in alternative medicine, having written several books. I flew down to stay a while with my mother and spend time with Jerry. I was to be hit with several shocks. Jerry had not just quit writing me—he thought I had quit writing him. The obvious conclusion was that my father, who had been out of work at the time, had stolen all the letters from both of us and had effectively broken us up. Next I realized that though Jerry retained the part of his brain that contained his intellect, he had reverted socially to a 14-year-old, chasing after women. Lastly, I found out he was married. I had a blow-up with my mother over her past behavior and she went crying to my sisters, who took her side. I was not in good shape when an invitation came from a cousin with a summer home on a large lake. I knew my cousin was pretty wild in her younger years, but thought she had settled down in her second marriage. She taught me how to ride a jet ski and then played follow the leader all over that huge lake, right down to the edge of the dam, creating a deep eddy threatening to suck me in, crossing the wake of a large boat, causing me to go airborne, etc. She had me out for five hours and I kept up with every move she made. I had a bad sunburn, which her family treated with apple cider vinegar. As I calmed down, I realized that what I had just experienced was another suicide attempt. I had taken a lot of stupid chances, any one of which could have killed me and part of me was hoping it would, but another part of me wanted to prove that I could ride as well as an expert my first time out. I'm not quite sure what was going through my cousin's mind.

Sam died in 1990 of leukemia. Neddie died in 2014—the only way I know that is from looking it up online.

My mother died in 2015. She had sold her house and was living with Beth, who took care of her as long as she could and finally put her in a nursing home. In her later years Ona was no longer able to maintain her false facade, so she turned into a screaming banshee, which was her true character. At the age of 92, she fell and broke her hip. The nursing home opted to keep her in bed, sedated, and she died two weeks later. I'm sure that was a relief to the nursing home staff. I did not go to the funeral.

EPILOGUE

Have I accomplished my two goals of writing this book? I suppose I have had some catharsis, though, of course, not complete relief. Both of my parents and husbands have passed on–I could not have written this otherwise. I have disguised names to avoid embarrassing anyone.

An integral part of the way I was treated was due to mental illness. I call bipolar the family curse, because of all those afflicted with it—my grandmother, my father, my sister, two nephews, and a cousin. But there are many people with bipolar who do not abuse others, so I don't see that as an excuse.

I know I must forgive all who have trespassed against me, if I wish to be forgiven of my trespasses–the Lord's Prayer says so. Is it possible to forgive without forgetting?

In the fifties there were no laws to protect children—they were considered to be property of the parents, like a piece of furniture—to be done with as the parents wished. My father used to threaten to send me to reform school. I assume that was probably a threat his bipolar mother used on him. Now I think that reform school would have been an improvement over my life, that is if they accepted A students with exemplary behavior.

I can only hope that the second goal will be accomplished, because that is up to you.

My prayer is still that it will be enough. The answer is that when I breathe my last breath on this earth—then it will be enough.

Printed in the United States
By Bookmasters